WILD WORK

Who Cleans Dinosaur Bones?

WORKING AT A MUSEUM

Margie Markarian

Raintree

Chicago, Illinois

www.heinemannraintree.com
Visit our website to find out
more information about
Heinemann-Raintree books.

To order:
☎ Phone 888-454-2279
💻 Visit www.heinemannraintree.com
to browse our catalog and order online.

© 2011 Raintree
an imprint of Capstone Global Library, LLC
Chicago, Illinois

Edited by David Andrews, Nancy Dickmann, and Rebecca
Rissman
Designed by Victoria Allen
Picture research by Liz Alexander
Leveled by Marla Conn, with Read-Ability.
Originated by Dot Gradations Ltd
Printed and bound in China by Leo Paper Products Ltd

15 14 13 12 11 10
10 9 8 7 6 5 4 3 2 1

Library of Congress Cataloging-in-Publication Data
Markarian, Margie.
  Who cleans dinosaur bones? : working at a museum / Margie
Markarian.
    p. cm. —(Wild work)
  Includes bibliographical references and index.
  ISBN 978-1-4109-3847-3 (hc)—ISBN 978-1-4109-3857-2
(pb) 1. Natural history museums—Employees—Juvenile
literature. 2. Taxidermists—Juvenile literature. 3. Taxidermy—
Juvenile literature. 4. Paleontologists—Juvenile literature. 5.
Natural history museum curators—Juvenile literature. I. Title.
  QH70.M367 2011
  069—dc22
                            2009050175

Acknowledgements
The author and publisher are grateful to the following for
permission to reproduce copyright material:

Alamy pp. **4** (© Guido Schiefer), **6** (© ilian animal), **7**
(© LondonPhotos), **10** (© David R. Frazier Photolibrary, Inc.),
16 (© Kevin Foy), **20** (© imagebroker), **24** (© Luscious
Frames), **29** (© Jeff Greenberg); Corbis pp. **5** (© Atlantide
Phototravel), **14** (© PHIL McCARTEN), **15** (© HO/Reuters),
18 (© Brooks Kraft), **22** (© Paul A. Souders), **23** (© Jan
Butchofsky-Houser), **26** (© Aaron M. Cohen), **27** (© Steve
Winter), **28** (© Randy Faris); Getty Images pp. **11** (Jean-Marc
Giboux), **12** (Harri Tahvanainen/Gorilla Creative Images),
13 (Matt Cardy), **17** (Chris Jackson), **19** (Tim Graham Photo
Library); Photolibrary p. **25** (sodapix/F1 Online); Science
Photo Library pp. **8** (Philippe Plailly), **9** (Philippe Plailly);
The Colonial Williamsburg Foundation **2008** p. **21**
(David M Doody).

Background design features reproduced with permission of
Shutterstock (© vgm).

Cover photograph reproduced with permission of Corbis
(© Bill Varie).

We would like to thank Mieka Sywak for her invaluable help
in the preparation of this book.

Every effort has been made to contact copyright holders of
any material reproduced in this book. Any omissions will
be rectified in subsequent printings if notice is given to
the publisher.

Some words are shown in bold, **like this.** You can find
out what they mean by looking in the glossary.

Contents

Floors to Explore

At museums you can go back in time. You can dance with a robot. You can talk to a person from history. You can take a trip to the moon. People who work at museums make all these adventures possible.

DID YOU KNOW?

There are more than 17,500 museums in the United States.

Collection Keepers

Museum **curators** (say *cue-RAY-tors*) are collectors. But they don't collect stuffed animals, trading cards, or action figures.

Some curators collect art or historic items. Others collect scientific objects. They can't put everything they collect on display. They choose items that will interest visitors and teach them new things.

On Display

Look at this **hologram**! It welcomes visitors to an **exhibit**, or display, at a science museum in Paris, France.

Exhibit designers create exciting
displays like this. They tell why
the displays are important and
how things work. Sometimes
the exhibits tell a story.

Who Cleans Those Big Bones?

It took 67 million years for this beast to rise again! She is a *Tyrannosaurus rex*, and her name is Sue.

DID YOU KNOW?

A T. Rex could crunch 500 pounds (227 kg) of meat in one big bite!

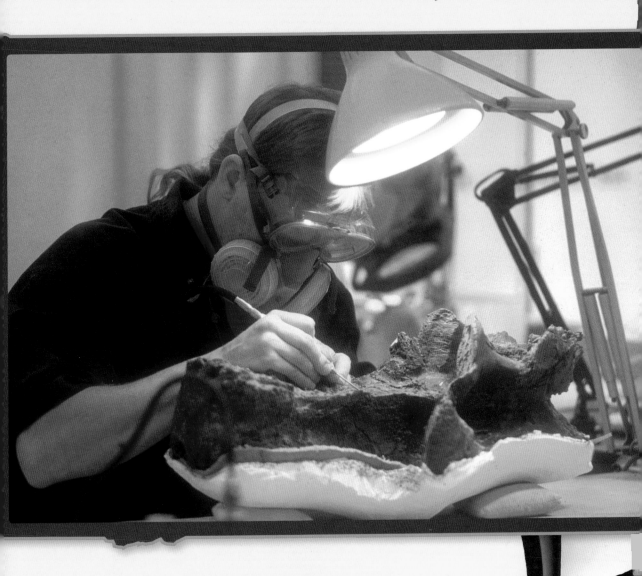

A team of **paleontologists**
(say *PAY-lee-un-TALL-oh-gists*)
dug Sue's bones out of the
ground. They used special tools
to clean the bones for display.

Entering the Dead Zone

Watch out! This tiger looks ready to pounce. It seems real because its skin and fur *are* real.

Taxidermists (say *TAX-uh-DURM-ists*) take skin from dead animals. They **preserve**, or save it and use it to make a model. Their work gives people a safe way to learn about animals up close.

Up to Their Eyeballs in Wax!

Some museums show models of people. They look just like famous people, but they are made of wax!

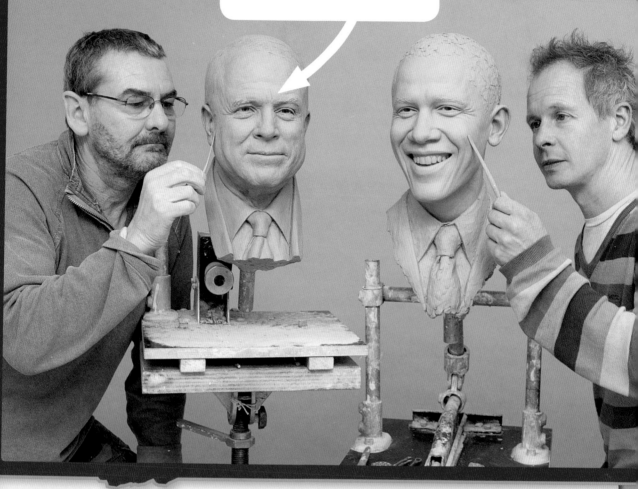

It takes four months to make one wax figure. Twenty people work together on it. To start, they need photos and more than 250 exact body and face measurements.

To make a head, the team shapes it from a blob of clay. They wait for the clay to harden. The clay face is used to create a **mold**, or a hollow container shaped like the head.

wax head

mold

Hot wax is poured into the mold. When it cools, it comes out in the shape of the head. Then it's time to paint lips, insert hair, and pop in plastic or glass eyeballs!

Acting the Part

At living history museums, workers pretend to be people from the past. They are **role players**.

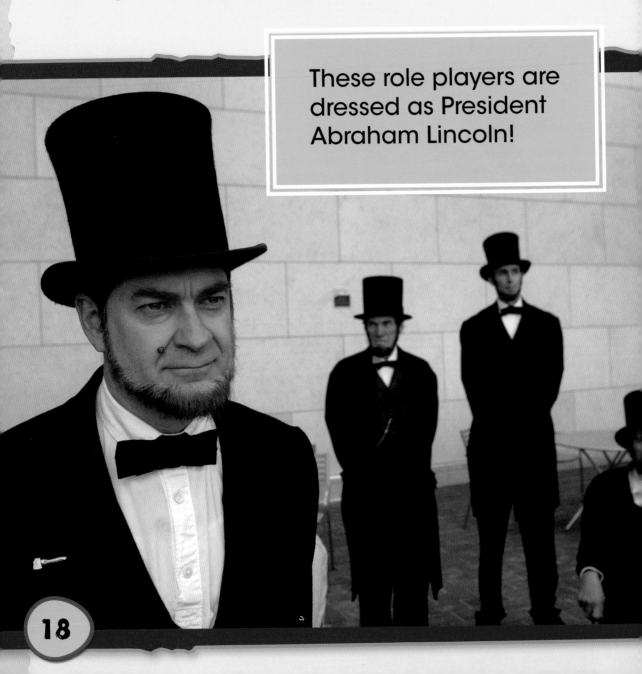

These role players are dressed as President Abraham Lincoln!

They dress up in costumes and act out history. They show and tell what life was like a long time ago.

Time-Travel Fashion

Who gives these **role players** something to wear? Costume managers do! Costume managers study fashions from the past. They make sure every button, buckle, and belt fits the time period.

DID YOU KNOW?
The costume department at Colonial Williamsburg takes care of more than 60,000 clothing items.

21

Now That's Crafty!

Ever wonder how people made dishes or clothes in the past? They had to work by hand. These museum workers show how crafts were made before machines or factories could make these items for people to buy.

This mans shows how blacksmiths used to make horseshoes.

This woman shows
how fabrics used
to be made.

Sound and Light Wizards

Audio-visual experts really know how to light up a room. They work to add light and sound to museum **exhibits**. They create lightning bolts in theaters of electricity. They switch on the stars in the night sky at **planetariums**.

A Night at the Museum

Museums are great places for parties. Special event planners help museums organize parties. Sometimes they arrange sleepovers for scouts, schools, and families.

These kids at New York's Museum of Natural History are sleeping under a blue whale!

Could You Work at a Museum?

If you love art, history, or science, you could work in a museum too.

Many museum workers start out as volunteers when they are in high school or college. These jobs aren't easy. But they can be a fun way to teach people more about the world.

Glossary

curator person who takes care of a museum's collections

exhibit a museum display of objects such as art or historic items

hologram special pattern of lights made to look like another object

mold hollow container used to shape objects

paleontologists scientists who study the fossils of living things

planetarium a building with equipment that can show images from space on a curved ceiling

preserve save an animal, plant, or object, usually with chemicals

role player person pretending to be someone else

taxidermist a person who makes stuffed animals from real animal skins

Find Out More

Books to Read

Mark, Jan. *The Museum Book: A Guide to Strange and Wonderful Collections.* Somerville, MA: Candlewick Press, 2007.

Web Sites to Visit

http://www.metmuseum.org/explore/Aarons_Awesome_Adventure/index.html

Read an online story about how a young boy's visits to an art museum changed his life.

http://www.smithsonianeducation.org/students/idealabs/smithsonian_kids.html

Take a kid-friendly virtual tour of the largest museum complex in the United States.

http://www.smithsonianeducation.org/students/smithsonian_kids_collecting/main.html

Learn about people who collect everything from snow globes to cowboy hats and what these collections have in common with museum collections.

Index